W9-ASR-819

DATE DUE

SP

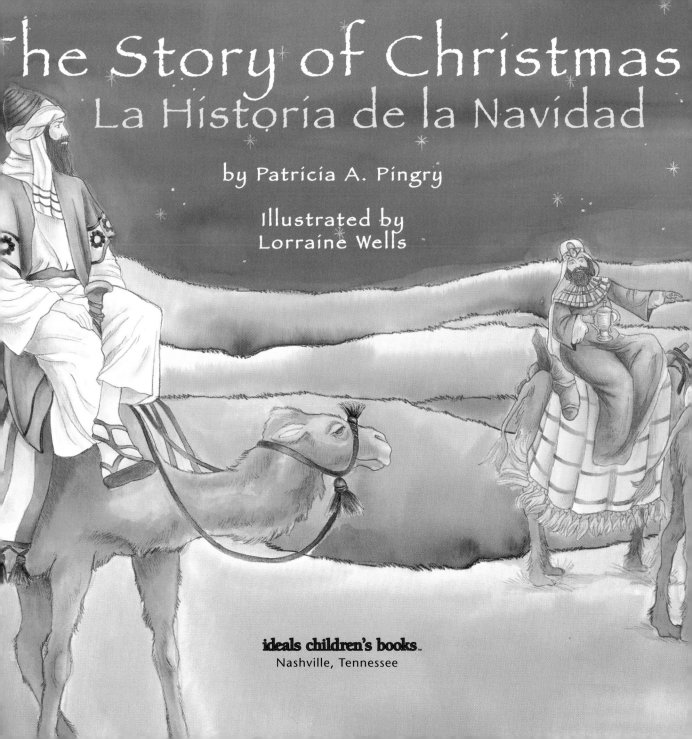

The Story of Christmas
La Historia de la Navidad

by Patricia A. Pingry

Illustrated by
Lorraine Wells

ideals children's books.
Nashville, Tennessee

ISBN 0-8249-4134-9

Published by Ideals Children's Books
An imprint of Ideals Publications, a division of Guideposts
535 Metroplex Drive, Suite 250, Nashville, Tennessee 37211
www.idealsbooks.com

Printed and bound in Mexico by RR Donnelley & Sons.

Library of Congress Cataloging-in-Publication Data

Pingry, Patricia.
    [Story of Christmas. Spanish & English]
    The story of Christmas = La historia de la Navidad / by Patricia A. Pingry ; illustrated by Lorraine Wells.
        p. cm.
    Summary: A bilingual description of the birth of Jesus and the reason for celebrating Christmas.
    ISBN 0-8249-4134-9 (alk. paper)
    1. Jesus Christ--Nativity--Juvenile literature. 2. Christmas--Juvenile literature. [1. Jesus Christ--Nativity. 2. Christmas. 3. Spanish language materials--Bilingual.] I. Title: Historia de la Navidad. II. Wells, Lorraine Schreiner, ill. III. Title.

    BT315.2 .P5518 2001
    232.92--dc21   2001035755

        5 7 9 10 8 6 4

To Parents and Teachers:

The Story of Christmas, La Historia de l Navidad, is one of a series of bilingua books specially created by Ideals Chil dren's Books to help children and thei parents learn to read both Spanish an English through a familiar Bible story.

If the child's first language is English he or she will understand and be able t read the text on the left-hand pages o this book. If the child wishes to read Span ish, he or she will be able to read the right hand pages of the book. Whether th child's native language is English or Span ish, he or she will be able to compare th text of the two pages and, thus, learn t read both English and Spanish.

Also included at the end of the stor are several common words listed in bot English and Spanish that the child ma view. These include both nouns, with heir gender in Spanish, and verbs. In the ase of the verbs, the Spanish verbs have ne endings that indicate their use in the :ory.

Parents and teachers will want to use his book as a beginning reader for children who speak either English or Spanish.

los Padres y los Maestros:

he Story of Christmas, La Historia de la Javidad es parte de una serie de libros bilngüe hecho especialmente por Ideals Children's Books para ayudar a los niños y sus padres a aprender como leer en los los idiomas, español e inglés, por medio de un cuento familiar de la Biblia.

Si el primer idioma del niño es inglés, él puede leer y entender lo que está escrito en la página a la izquierda. Si el niño quiere leer en español, él puede leer las páginas a la derecha. Cualquiera que sea el idioma nativo, el inglés o el español, el niño podrá comparar lo escrito en las dos páginas y entonces aprenderá como leer en inglés y en español.

Al final de la historia es incluida para repasar una lista de varias palabras comunes en el inglés y el español. La lista tiene ambos nombres, con el género y verbos en español con los fines que indican el uso en la historia.

Los padres y los maestros tendrán ganas de usar este librito como libro principio para niños que hablan inglés o español.

Do you know why we give gifts at Christmas?
We give presents because it is Jesus' birthday.

¿Sabes por qué damos regalos en Navidad?
Intercambiamos regalos en esa fecha porque
es el cumpleaños de Jesús.

Long ago, an angel told Mary she would have
a Baby named Jesus.

Hace mucho tiempo, un ángel le dijo a María
que iba a tener un Niño, llamado Jesús.

Mary and her husband, Joseph, were very happy. They had a lot to do to get ready for the Baby.

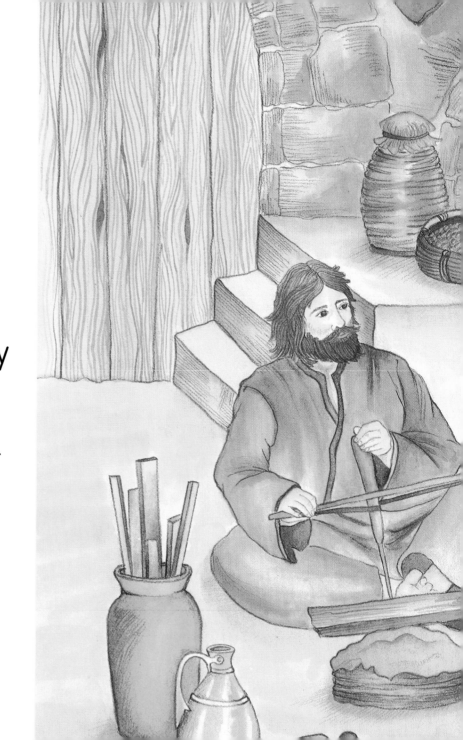

María y su esposo, José, estaban muy felices. Tenían mucho que preparar para la llegada del Niño.

First, they had to take a long trip to Bethlehem.
Mary rode a donkey; Joseph walked.

Primero, tenían que hacer un viaje largo a Belén.

María viajó en burro. José caminó.

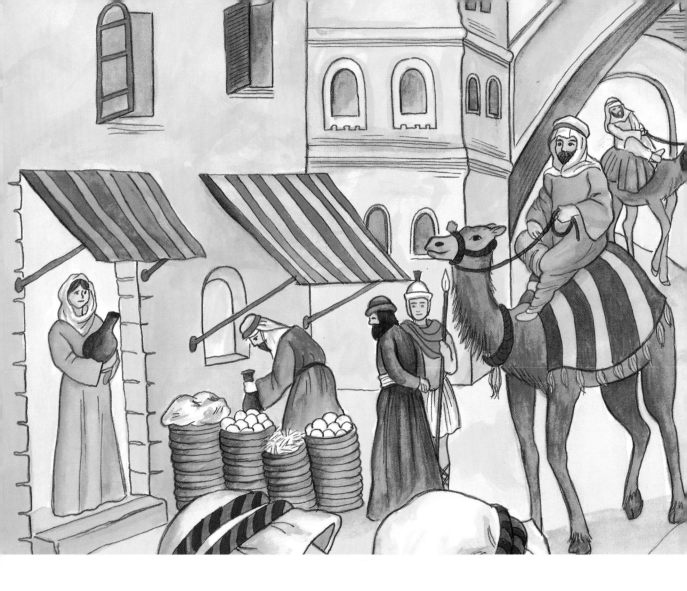

When they got to Bethlehem,
many people were there.

Cuando llegaron a Belén,
había mucha gente en la ciudad.

Mary and
Joseph were
very tired,
but there was
no place for
them to stay.

María y José
estaban muy
cansados;
pero no tenían
ningún lugar
donde
hospedarse.

They slept on a bed of hay in a stable with a cow and the donkey.

Durmieron en una cama de heno en un establo, con una vaca y el burro.

That night, Baby
Jesus was born.

Esa noche, nació el Niño Jesús.

Angels told the shepherds, "Jesus is born!
You will find Him in a manger."

Los ángeles le dijeron a los pastores: "Hoy nació
esús. Encontrarán ustedes al Niño en un pesebre."

Wise men followed a star
to the stable and Baby Jesus.

Los Reyes Magos siguieron una estrella hasta el establo y encontraron al Niño Jesús.

They all brought Baby Jesus presents
because they loved Him.

Todos le llevaron regalos al Niño Jesús
porque lo amaban.

We give gifts at Christmas
to show our love

Nosotros damos regalos en Navidad
para mostrar nuestro amor

and to say, "Happy birthday, Baby Jesus."

y para decir: "Feliz cumpleaños, Niño Jesús."

Vocabulary words used in

The Story of Christmas
La Historia de la Navidad

English	Spanish	English	Spanish
story	la historia	her	su
Christmas	la Navidad	husband	el esposo
you know	sabes	very	muy
why	por qué	a lot	mucho
we give	damos	to prepare	preparar
gifts	los regalos	arrival	la llegada
at	en	first	primero
because	porque	long	largo
it is	es	trip	el viaje
Jesus	Jesús	Bethlehem	Belén
angel	el ángel	donkey	el burro
he told	dijo	he walked	caminó
to have	tener	when	cuando
baby	el niño	they arrived	llegaron
named	llamado	people	la gente
and	y	city	la ciudad

English	Spanish	English	Spanish
they were	estaban	today	hoy
tired	cansado	you (plural)	ustedes
but	pero	manger	el pesebre
place	el lugar	wise men	los Reyes Magos
to stay	hospedarse	they followed	siguieron
they slept	durmieron	star	la estrella
bed	la cama	all	todos
hay	el heno	they brought	llevaron
stable	el establo	they loved him	lo amaban
with	con	to show	mostrar
cow	la vaca	our	nuestro
that	esa	love	el amor
night	la noche	to say	decir
he was born	nació	happy	feliz
shepherds	los pastores	birthday	el cumpleaños